TAX Cafe®

Taxcafe Tax Guides

# How to Tap Your IRA or 401(k) and Escape Tax

## The 60 Minute Guide to the Early Withdrawal Rules

By Nick Braun EA PhD

ISBN 978-1-906888-02-2
First Edition, February 2009



Taxcafe books are available at special quantity discounts to use for sale promotions, employee premiums, or educational purposes. For more information, please e-mail our Sales Department at sales@taxcafe.com.

For more information about Taxcafe publications, visit our web site at www.taxcafe.com.

Published by Taxcafe Ltd, 67 Milton Road, Kirkcaldy, KY1 1TL, UK

## Limit of Liability/Disclaimer of Warranty

## About the Author

The author is Nick Braun EA PhD. Nick is the founder of Taxcafe.com and has been involved in the tax publishing world since 1989 as a writer, editor and publisher.

He is an Enrolled Agent licensed to represent taxpayers before the IRS, and is a member of the National Association of Enrolled Agents and the National Association of Tax Professionals.

He also holds a PhD in economics and is a columnist for several investment and business magazines.

## *Dedication*

Once again, to Aileen for all your love and support and to Jake, Sandy and Tilly for all the joy you bring.

## *Thanks*

Thank you to my parents, Ann and Deryck, for all your encouragement over the years. I would also like to thank my in-laws, Douglas and June, for the tremendous help and support you have given us over the past 10 years.

# Contents

# Introduction

A growing number of people are using their retirement plans as a source of emergency cash.

According to a poll by the Wall Street Journal Online/Harris Interactive, one quarter of US adults withdraw funds before retirement and almost half never pay the money back.

The most common reason for making an early withdrawal is to pay the bills when a family member loses a job, or to make a down payment on a home.

Withdrawing money from an IRA or 401(k) before you retire should always be seen as a last resort. What you spend today will be gone tomorrow... when you will probably need the money more than ever!

It should also be remembered that retirement plans enjoy an extremely powerful tax break – tax-free compounding. Every dollar you withdraw early will permanently lose this special treatment.

With tax-free compounding $1 could grow to $4.31 in 20 years time, assuming investment growth of 8% per year. Without tax-free compounding that same dollar might only grow to $2.61.

So money inside an IRA or 401(k) plan should always be treated as special and left alone if possible.

That is why you should always try to find emergency cash elsewhere, either by taking a loan from a bank or family member or by selling other assets.

Having said that, a growing number of households, struggling under the weight of large credit card bills and shrinking home equity, are being forced to dip into their retirement savings to help them through difficult economic times.

This guide explains in plain English the rules for withdrawing money early from traditional IRAs, Roth IRAs and 401(k) plans and highlights some of the traps you should watch out for.

## Income Taxes

If you withdraw money early from a traditional IRA or 401(k) plan you will almost always pay income tax on the whole amount. You could also end up paying an extra 10% early distribution tax.

So if you withdraw $10,000 and your income tax rate is 28%, you will have to pay $2,800 in Federal income tax as well as a $1,000 early distribution tax, leaving you with just $6,200 and possibly even less if you also owe state income tax.

Often there is not much you can do to avoid regular income tax on retirement plan withdrawals. There is, however, lots you can do to avoid the 10% early distribution tax. A substantial portion of this guide is devoted to explaining these tax-saving techniques.

Chapter 1 deals with early withdrawals from traditional IRAs and Chapter 5 covers 401(k) plans.

Unlike IRAs, most 401(k) plans allow you to take a loan. Borrowing money from your 401(k) plan allows you to avoid both income tax and the 10% early withdrawal charge.

Eventually the money will be repaid and resume tax-free compounding again. Chapter 5 also explains how much you can borrow and looks at the pros and cons.

## Substantially Equal Periodic Payments

Probably the most appealing way to extract cash permanently from a traditional IRA or 401(k) plan, without the 10% penalty, is to take "substantially equal periodic payments" (SEPPs). These are regular annual withdrawals which have to last for at least five years.

When it comes to SEPP plans IRAs are the most flexible of all because your employment status does not matter. With an employer plan, like a 401(k), you can only start taking these regular payments once your employment is terminated.

Because of the usefulness and complexity of these SEPP plans, the whole of Chapter 2 is devoted to explaining their rules.

Roth IRAs are arguably a much better source of emergency cash than traditional IRAs and 401(k) plans and it is possible to take significant withdrawals without having to pay any income tax or the 10% additional tax.

If you have converted a traditional IRA into a Roth IRA you have to be careful to avoid certain traps if you withdraw any money within the first five years.

The Roth withdrawal rules are explained in detail in Chapter 4, with easy to follow examples.

Some people tap their retirement savings to start a business. It is possible in certain circumstances to fund a new business venture from your retirement plan without making a taxable distribution.

Essentially you get your retirement plan to buy stock in the business. The money your retirement plan pays for the stock then goes directly into the business bank account.

It's a somewhat gray area of the tax code, but if you set it all up properly you will effectively be able to withdraw money without paying either income tax or the 10% early distribution tax.

This issue is covered briefly in Chapter 1.

Finally, in Chapter 6 we take a look at the reporting requirements for early withdrawals, in particular the forms you may have to complete and submit with your tax return.

I hope you find this guide interesting and useful!

*Nick Braun EA, PhD*

# 1

# Tapping Your Traditional IRA

It is usually easier to withdraw money early from an IRA than a 401(k). As long as you are prepared to pay the 10% early withdrawal tax, you can take out your money at any time and for any reason.

With 401(k) plans the rules are slightly different. Every employer's plan has a different set of rules and some plans are more restrictive than others.

Both types of plan, however, allow you to withdraw money without the 10% penalty in certain situations.

In this chapter we will look at when traditional IRA withdrawals escape the 10% penalty tax. After that we will look at Roth IRAs and 401(k) plans.

## SIMPLE IRAs

If you have a SIMPLE IRA (an employer provided retirement plan) there is one extra rule to remember.

For SIMPLE IRAs the 10% additional tax is increased to 25% if the individual receives a distribution within two years of making the first contribution to the SIMPLE IRA account.

After two years the penalty falls back to 10%.

Members of SIMPLE IRAs can, however, avoid either the 10% or 25% penalty if they qualify for any of the exceptions listed in this chapter.

## How to Avoid the 10% Penalty

IRA withdrawals can be made without the 10% early withdrawal tax in the following circumstances (remember, however, that regular income tax will still be payable):

### When You Turn 59½

Most IRA account holders know that they can start taking money out when they reach age 59½. Nevertheless it is worth mentioning for completeness.

Withdrawals after age 59½ escape the 10% early distribution tax, withdrawals before age 59½ are subject to the 10% tax… unless you qualify for one of the exceptions listed below.

Note that you have to be at least 59½ on the day you make the withdrawal. If you only reach age 59½ later in the year, you do not escape the 10% tax.

## When You Die

It's not much consolation, but if you die before you are 59½, your beneficiary will not have to pay the 10% early withdrawal penalty.

It is also possible for your spouse-beneficiary to roll over a distribution from your retirement plan or IRA to his or her retirement plan or IRA.

## Permanent Disability

Also small consolation, if you become permanently disabled money can be withdrawn from your IRA without the 10% penalty.

So what is meant by disability?

If a physician decides that due to mental or physical disability you are unable to do the type of work you were doing before you were disabled, you are allowed to take penalty-free distributions from your IRA.

If you can still do some type of work – but not the same type you customarily do – you may still qualify for this exception. For example, a surgeon who damages his hand and can no longer operate may qualify.

The disability must be expected to last *permanently* or, at the risk of sounding morbid, result in your death.

These distributions can be used for any purpose.

## Medical Expenses

If you have non-reimbursed medical expenses you can make penalty-free IRA withdrawals to cover the costs. The expenses can be for you, your spouse or dependent.

There is a big catch, however. Your withdrawals are only penalty free to the extent your medical expenses exceed 7.5% of your adjusted gross income (AGI).

## Example

Tom is 45 years old and has AGI of $50,000 and medical expenses of $5,000, paid for using a distribution from his IRA. His calculation looks like this:

| | |
|---|---|
| Adjusted gross income | $50,000 |
| Medical expenses | $5,000 |
| 7.5% AGI | $3,750 |
| Excess | $1,250 |

Only $1,250 will avoid the 10% penalty. The 10% penalty is payable on the remaining $3,750.

Remember also that regular income tax has to be paid on the entire $5,000 early distribution.

This exception is available for both IRAs and 401(k)s.

**Tax Busting Tip!**

The medical expenses exception is available to everybody, not just those who itemize expenses on their tax returns. If you claim the standard deduction you still qualify.

### Health Insurance Premiums

This exception is unique to IRAs and is not available on 401(k) plans.

If you lose your job you can use money in your IRA to pay your medical insurance premiums for yourself, your spouse and your dependents.

You can only do this if:

- You have received state or Federal unemployment compensation for 12 consecutive weeks at least.
- You received the money from your IRA during the same year you received unemployment compensation, or the following year.
- The IRA money is received not more than 60 days after you return to work.

All three conditions have to be met to qualify.

Self-employed individuals will also qualify for penalty-free distributions if they would have received unemployment compensation except for the fact that they were self-employed.

**First-time Home Purchase**

This exception to the 10% additional tax is available for IRAs but not 401(k) plans.

The 10% early distribution tax is waived if you are a first-time homebuyer and withdraw money from your IRA to pay house purchase expenses.

Either you, your spouse, parent, grandparent, child or grandchild can be the first-time homebuyer.

There's a lifetime limit of $10,000 for this exception.

However, the whole $10,000 does not have to be taken at once. For example, you could withdraw $5,000 for one child this year and $5,000 for another child next year.

If both you and your spouse are first-time homebuyers **each** of you can receive up to $10,000 without having to pay the 10% additional tax.

The money must be used within 120 days of being paid out. If something goes wrong and the home purchase is cancelled or delayed, the money can be repaid to your IRA within 120 days without penalty.

Be careful of going over the 120 day limit, however. There have been cases where this has happened, through no fault of the taxpayer, and the 10% additional tax has had to be paid on the whole distribution, resulting in an extra tax bill of $1,000!

The money must be used to buy your "principal residence". The IRS usually defines this as the home you live in most of the time. So vacation homes and other second properties would not qualify.

Acceptable costs include:

- The costs of buying, building, or rebuilding a home.

- The usual settlement, financing and closing costs.

The money cannot be used to make regular mortgage payments.

**Tax Busting Tip!**

It does not have to be your first ever home purchase. A first-time home buyer is someone who has not owned a principal residence in the last two years. If you are married, neither of you is allowed to have owned a principal residence during the last two years.

### Higher Education Costs

This exception applies to IRAs but not 401(k) plans.

Certain higher education costs for you, your spouse, children and grandchildren can be paid out of your IRA savings without penalty, providing:

- The money is used to pay for tuition, books, supplies and equipment. The money can also be used to pay room and board if the student is enrolled at least half time in a degree program.
- The expenses are paid on behalf of you, the IRA owner, your spouse child or grandchild.
- The distribution does not exceed the expenses.

**Tax Busting Tip!**

You do not have to use your IRA money to actually pay the education costs. It's OK if the costs were paid using:

- A loan or gift.
- An inheritance given to either the student or the IRA account holder.
- Your personal savings (including savings from a qualified tuition program.

However, you cannot avoid the 10% early distribution tax if the education expenses were paid with:

- Tax-free distributions from a Coverdell savings account
- The tax-free part of scholarships/fellowships
- Pell grants
- Employer-provided educational assistance
- Veterans' educational assistance
- Any other tax-free payment (other than a gift or inheritance) received as educational assistance.

Eligible educational institutions include colleges, universities, vocational schools, or other postsecondary educational institutions eligible to participate in the Department of Education's student aid programs.

Virtually all accredited postsecondary institutions qualify. The educational institution should be able to tell you if it is eligible.

## IRS Levy

The 10% penalty is waived if money is paid out of your IRA as a result of an IRS levy.

Note that you will not qualify for this exception if you voluntarily withdraw the money from your IRA to pay taxes in order to avoid a levy.

## Child Support & Alimony

Money withdrawn from your IRA for child support or alimony as part of a court-ordered qualified domestic relations order (QDRO) does NOT qualify for an exception to the 10% early distribution tax.

401(k) plans do qualify but IRAs do not.

Even if a court order forces you to pay child support or alimony out of your IRA you will still have to pay the 10% early distribution tax.

**Tax Busting Tip!**

There is a way to avoid the penalty if your spouse is entitled to some of your IRA as part of a written divorce agreement. It is possible to have funds deposited in an IRA in your spouse's name without paying the 10% penalty.

It's essential the funds are not paid to your spouse before they are placed in an IRA.

This strategy would not work for child support – these payments cannot be transferred into an IRA.

### Substantially Equal Periodic Payments (SEPPs)

If you do not qualify for any of the above exceptions or need to tap your IRA for more money, the easiest way to avoid the 10% additional tax is by setting up a SEPP plan.

SEPP is short for substantially equal periodic payments. This is a series of regular annual payments, calculated using IRS formulas.

Because this is such an important tax saving technique we've devoted the whole of the next chapter to explaining it.

## Tapping Your IRA to Fund a Business

You do not have to invest your IRA savings in stocks and bonds. You can also put your money into more "exotic" investments including:

- Real estate
- Private businesses

So if you want to tap your IRA to fund an exciting new business venture, you may be able to put cash from your retirement plan *directly* into the business, without having to withdraw it first and pay income tax and the 10% penalty.

Instead of making a withdrawal, you can get your retirement plan to buy stock in the business instead. The business in return gets the cash it needs to grow.

There are potentially even greater tax savings to be had further down the road: if you sell the business one day, your retirement plan may be entitled to a juicy tax-free windfall.

So far so good but there are lots of traps to watch out for when you invest your IRA cash in any business that is owned by you or your close family.

In fact, this seems to be an extremely gray area of the tax code. The IRS has issued a huge number of private letter rulings authorizing retirement accounts to fund private businesses but has not issued any general guidelines.

Remember private letter rulings apply to a specific taxpayer's case only. They cannot be relied upon by other taxpayers.

The IRS wants your retirement plan to be used to build a retirement nest egg and is concerned that you will try to get your hands on any money injected into a business or try to benefit in other ways.

In particular, you have to watch out for Section 4975 of the tax code which deals with "prohibited transactions".

If your IRA is involved in a prohibited transaction it will lose its tax-exempt status. This means you will have to pay income tax and the 10% penalty on your entire account.

A prohibited transaction is one which takes place between your IRA and a "disqualified person".

Disqualified persons include:

- The owner of the IRA account – YOU
- Your wife or husband
- Your children and grandchildren
- Parents and grandparents
- Any entity more than 50% owned by you or any of the above relatives.

Friends, business associates and brothers and sisters are not included on the prohibited list.

So the basic rule is you can only invest your IRA money in your business if you and your closest relatives own less than 50% of that business.

If your IRA invests in a business in which you already own 50% or more it will be a prohibited transaction and will cause your IRA to be nuked!

It also seems that you cannot be the key employee and key investor in the business. Basically, someone else has to have the right to hire or fire you.

The IRS wants to make sure you are not "self-dealing" or moving retirement funds in a way that might benefit you right now, by taking a salary or other immediate payment.

**Important Exception**

There is, however, widespread acceptance that an exemption exists for *new ventures*. A simultaneous investment by you and your IRA in the initial capitalization of a business may escape a prohibited transaction ruling.

This view is based on the so-called Swanson decision, an important tax case which those who promote self-directed or "check book" IRAs have come to rely on.

However, because of all the uncertainty it is probably wise to get approval of your specific plan from the IRS, which judges them on a case-by-case basis.

Furthermore, if you want to invest only some of your IRA savings in the business, it is probably advisable to first transfer that money into a separate IRA. This will ensure that, if you get hit by the prohibited transaction rules, your other IRA money will not be annihilated by taxes and penalties.

But most important of all, get help from a professional! There are several companies which specialize in administering self-directed IRAs and know the whole score. These include:

- Pensco Trust Company – penscotrust.com
- Trust Administration Services – trustlynk.com
- Guidant Financial Group – guidantfinancial.com
- Equity Trust Company – trustetc.com

You could be looking at fairly significant fees – maybe $4,000 to $5,000 or more to set up the necessary structures and obtain an IRS ruling. There will also be annual fees of around $1,000.

# 2

# *Substantially Equal Periodic Payments*

## Introduction

Anyone under 59½ can tap their IRA without the 10% additional tax by taking substantially equal periodic payments (SEPPs).

Everyone qualifies for this loophole: it doesn't matter how old you are or what you use the money for.

A SEPP plan is a series of regular payments (at least one a year) calculated using one of three IRS formulas.

You can choose whichever formula produces the most desirable annual payment. And each formula can be tweaked a bit to produce a bigger of smaller payment.

SEPP payments from your employer's plan can only begin after you leave your job. SEPP payments from traditional IRAs, however, can be taken at any time.

You still have to pay income tax on these early withdrawals but escape the 10% additional tax.

You can also elect not to have Federal income tax withheld from your SEPP payments (although you may then be responsible for estimated tax payments).

## The Five Year Minimum Rule

Under the SEPP rules you have to continue taking payments for at least five years or until you reach age 59½ – **whichever is longer**.

So if you are 40 years old you will have to continue taking these payments for almost 20 years, until you are 59½.

And if you are 57 you will have to continue taking these payments, not just until you are 59½, but for five years, at which time you will be 62.

## No Stopping or Changing

You cannot stop or reduce SEPP payments if your financial position improves or changes. If you do there are big penalties – the 10% additional tax on ALL the withdrawals you have made… plus interest!

You may, however, be able to make a one-time change in the way you calculate your payments. By switching formulas you can reduce your annual withdrawals and leave more money in your retirement plan.

One way to avoid withdrawing too much of your retirement savings is to split your IRA before you start your SEPP plan.

Work out how much you need to withdraw and put that into one IRA. Invest the rest in another IRA where it will continue to benefit from tax-free compounding until you retire.

Always seek professional advice before you do this.

SEPPs do not allow you to get your hands on a huge chunk of your retirement plan savings in one go. You will probably not be able to extract more than, say, 5% of your account balance each year.

Because you can only withdraw a small portion of your money each year and have to keep up your withdrawals for at least five years, SEPP plans are most suitable for those who require *ongoing* financial assistance.

For example, a SEPP plan could be suitable for someone who wants to retire early or someone with a new business that needs financial support for several years, or someone who needs ongoing help with loan repayments.

## Calculating Your SEPP Payments

There are three ways to calculate SEPP payments, also known as 72(t) payments:

- Required minimum distribution method
- Amortization method
- Annuitization method

Each method produces a different payment, although the amortization and annuitization methods produce payments of a broadly similar size.

If you start off with the amortization or annuitization method you can switch to the required minimum distribution method in a subsequent year.

However, once you make this change you must stick with it from then on.

You do not have to use any of these three formulas but they are IRS "safe harbors" which means that, as long as you follow them to the book, you will escape the 10% penalty.

You can use other methods but the IRS may disagree with your calculations and levy the 10% additional tax plus interest. You should not use another method without first obtaining a private letter ruling.

A private letter ruling is a written decision by the IRS in response to a taxpayer's specific request for guidance. They can cost thousands of dollars to prepare.

## Required Minimum Distribution Method

The required minimum distribution (RMD) method is the simplest way of calculating substantially equal periodic payments but also the least flexible.

To calculate it all you do is divide your retirement plan account balance by your life expectancy.

The annual payment is recalculated each year and could vary significantly if your investments have gone up or down in value.

### Example

John's IRA account balance is $100,000 and, because he turns 40 this year, his life expectancy is 43.6 years.

Dividing $100,000 by 43.6 gives us $2,294. This is the amount he must withdraw from his IRA this year using the required minimum distribution method.

He has to pay regular income tax on the whole amount but will escape the 10% penalty tax.

Next year his account balance may be $105,000 and because he is one year older his life expectancy will be 42.7 years. His required withdrawal will then be $2,459 ($105,000/42.7).

Although this technique is called the required *minimum* distribution method, the amount calculated is the *exact* amount you must withdraw.

If you distribute more or less this will result in a "busted" SEPP plan and you will have to pay the 10% additional tax plus interest on *all* distributions taken since the plan was set up.

## Calculating Your Account Balance

Of course, your retirement plan's account balance changes every day as the value of your stocks and bonds goes up and down. So what figure should you use for the calculation?

According to IRS publications it is acceptable to use your account balance on December 31 of the *previous* year.

So if John in the above example starts making substantially equal periodic payments on June 30, 2009 he can use his account balance on December 31, 2008.

And when he calculates his 2010 distribution he will use his account balance on December 31, 2009, and so on.

The IRS is also generally happy for you to use your account balance on any date between December 31 and the day you start withdrawing money.

So John in the above example could probably use his IRA account balance on any date from December 31, 2008 to June 30, 2009.

For subsequent years he can use the value either on December 31 of the prior year or any date within a reasonable period before that year's distribution.

If your account balance has changed due to market fluctuations, choosing the right date could have a big impact on the amount you can withdraw.

## Determining Your Life Expectancy

The other important number in the calculation is your life expectancy. So where do you find it?

The IRS publishes three tables you can use:

- Single life expectancy table
- Uniform life table or
- Joint life table (if you have a beneficiary)

You can find these tables in IRS publication 590 *Individual Retirement Arrangements*. The easiest way to find this publication is to type "IRS p590" into a search engine like Google.

You can use whichever life expectancy table produces the most desirable result for you. For example, the single life expectancy table will produce the biggest payment and can be used by married taxpayers.

If you use the joint life expectancy table then the person whose life expectancy you use must be your actual beneficiary (if you have more than one, use the oldest).

If you use the single life or uniform life table it is important to note that you must continue using that table in all subsequent years.

If you use the joint life table and a beneficiary dies or ceases to be a beneficiary or ceases to be the oldest beneficiary, you have to make a change for the next year of calculation. Use the oldest beneficiary or if there is none use the single life table.

## Determining Your Age

So what age should you plug into the life expectancy tables? According to the IRS you use the age *you will attain* during the year you take the distribution.

So if you are 45 years old when you calculate your distribution in June but turn 46 in December, you should use 46 as your age in the calculation.

## Sample Payments

Table 1 gives you a good idea of the level of payment you can expect in year 1 if you use the required minimum distribution method for your SEPP plan.

The sample payments are calculated by dividing the IRA account balance by life expectancy. The single life table was used because it produces the biggest payment. The table is reproduced in Appendix 1.

For example, if you are 45 years old and have $100,000 in your IRA, your life expectancy is 38.8 and you can withdraw $2,577 ($100,000/38.8).

**Table 1**
**Required Minimum Distribution Method**
***Sample Payments***

| Account Balance | Age 35 | 40 | 45 | 50 | 55 |
|---|---|---|---|---|---|
| $25,000 | 515 | 573 | 644 | 731 | 845 |
| $35,000 | 722 | 803 | 902 | 1,023 | 1,182 |
| $50,000 | 1,031 | 1,147 | 1,289 | 1,462 | 1,689 |
| $75,000 | 1,546 | 1,720 | 1,933 | 2,193 | 2,534 |
| $100,000 | 2,062 | 2,294 | 2,577 | 2,924 | 3,378 |
| $200,000 | 4,124 | 4,587 | 5,155 | 5,848 | 6,757 |
| $250,000 | 5,155 | 5,734 | 6,443 | 7,310 | 8,446 |
| $300,000 | 6,186 | 6,881 | 7,732 | 8,772 | 10,135 |
| $400,000 | 8,247 | 9,174 | 10,309 | 11,696 | 13,514 |
| $500,000 | 10,309 | 11,468 | 12,887 | 14,620 | 16,892 |

In year 2 your life expectancy will be a bit lower which will increase your payment but your IRA balance could be higher or lower depending on how well your investments have performed.

So it is impossible to say whether you will be able to take a bigger or smaller payment in the years ahead.

Probably the only way to ensure your payments remain relatively stable from year to year is to ensure your retirement plan money is invested in low-risk interest-bearing securities.

### Benefits & Drawbacks of the RMD Method

The biggest advantage of this method is simplicity – it is extremely easy to calculate the amount you have to withdraw each year.

This is the only method that results in payments that change from year to year – the amortization and annuitization methods produce annual payments that are permanently fixed.

One problem with the required minimum distribution method is your payments may be smaller in the early years (when you may want them to be big) and larger in later years, as your life expectancy falls. That's not helpful if you need income now!

Furthermore, if you need to tap your retirement plan for as much cash as possible be warned that the required minimum distribution method can produce an annual payment only half as big as the amortization and annuitization methods.

## The Amortization Method

If you want to withdraw as much as possible from your retirement plan you should consider the amortization method.

This method is also popular because it is flexible – allowing you to tweak the formula and pick from a range of payments.

However, once you pick a payment it must remain fixed from that point on.

Your annual withdrawal is calculated using 3 things:

- **An interest rate**. You can choose any interest rate as long as it is not more than 120% of the "mid-term Applicable Federal Rate".

  You can use the rate for *either* of the two months preceding the month you begin distributions.

  You can find these rates at www.72t.net. At the time of writing the maximum rate was 3.43%. The higher the interest rate you use, the higher your payment.

- **Your Life Expectancy**. You can use the same three tables available for the required minimum distribution method. Again you can find these in the Appendices of IRS Publication 590 (simply type "IRS Publication 590" into a search engine like Google).

- **Your Account Balance**. Again you can take the value of your account on December 31 of the *preceding* year or any time between then and your first withdrawal. If your account balance has changed due to market fluctuations, choosing the right date could have a big impact on the amount you can withdraw.

You can calculate the distribution under the amortization method yourself using a financial calculator but it's much easier to use one of the free calculators available online because they do everything for you.

To find these free calculators type "SEPP calculator" into Google and you'll find various well-known websites including:

- www.72t.net
- fidelity.com
- cch.com

For example, www.72t.net has a calculator which you will find by clicking the "Calculators" button on the homepage and selecting the "SEPP 72(t)" option.

**Example**

Let's say Steve is 50 and has $100,000 in his IRA. He wants to withdraw the maximum amount possible so he uses the maximum interest rate allowed which was 3.43% at the time of writing.

Plugging those numbers into an online calculator produces an annual payment of $5,011 using the amortization method.

The minimum distribution method produces an annual payment of $2,924, so clearly the amortization method is the better option for someone wanting to extract cash quickly from a retirement plan.

Steve's payment for the next and future years will also be $5,011. In fact, he has to withdraw this amount each year until he reaches age 59½.

He will have to pay income tax on these withdrawals but escapes the 10% early withdrawal penalty.

If he requires less money he can use a smaller interest rate in the initial calculation or he could speak to his financial adviser about splitting his IRA money into two accounts, using one for withdrawals and investing one for his retirement.

72t.net has a useful reverse calculator that works out how much money you need to allocate to produce your desired monthly payment.

## Sample Payments

Table 2 gives you an idea of the level of payment you can expect every year if you use the amortization method for your SEPP plan.

(Note that these sample payments may already be out of date when you read this because they are based on interest rates that were current at the time of writing.)

The single life expectancy table was used for the calculations because it produces the biggest payment.

For example, if you are 45 years old and have $100,000 in your IRA, your annual payment would be $4,700.

This amount must be withdrawn from your IRA every year until you reach age 59½.

## Table 2
### Amortization Method
*Sample Payments*

| Account Balance | Age 35 | 40 | 45 | 50 | 55 |
|---|---|---|---|---|---|
| $25,000 | 1,065 | 1,113 | 1,175 | 1,253 | 1,358 |
| $35,000 | 1,491 | 1,559 | 1,645 | 1,754 | 1,901 |
| $50,000 | 2,130 | 2,227 | 2,350 | 2,506 | 2,716 |
| $75,000 | 3,195 | 3,340 | 3,525 | 3,759 | 4,074 |
| $100,000 | 4,260 | 4,454 | 4,700 | 5,011 | 5,432 |
| $200,000 | 8,520 | 8,907 | 9,400 | 10,023 | 10,863 |
| $250,000 | 10,650 | 11,134 | 11,750 | 12,529 | 13,579 |
| $300,000 | 12,780 | 13,361 | 14,100 | 15,034 | 16,295 |
| $400,000 | 17,040 | 17,814 | 18,800 | 20,046 | 21,727 |
| $500,000 | 21,300 | 22,268 | 23,500 | 25,057 | 27,158 |

**Notes:**
Based on interest rate of 3.43%
Life expectancy calculated using single life table

## Modifying Amortization Method Payments

Once you have done the initial calculation you do not do it again – your payments have to remain fixed for five years or until you reach age 59½, whichever is longer.

If you stop or modify them the IRS will force you to pay the 10% additional tax on ALL the withdrawals you have taken... plus interest.

Having said that, there are some favorable private letter rulings which have allowed taxpayers to recalculate their amortization method payment each year.

Recalculating could help you increase your annual payment. At present, interest rates are at historic lows and many taxpayers have seen their retirement account balances shrink thanks to the 2008 collapse on Wall Street.

So the maximum withdrawal you can take today using the amortization method is possibly a lot lower than the distribution you could have taken in, say, 2007.

For example, our 45 year old with $100,000 would only be able to withdraw $4,700 today compared with approximately $11,000 when interest rates were higher and stocks were at their peaks.

For recalculation to succeed the recalculation should be included as part of the *original* plan submitted to your retirement plan custodian. It's probably too late too consider implementing if your SEPP plan is already up and running.

Recalculating your amortization payments without obtaining your own private letter ruling could be extremely risky but unfortunately private letter rulings are costly to obtain.

So you should only consider this option if you think the benefits of a significantly higher distribution outweigh the costs of obtaining a ruling.

Seek professional advice before you act!

### Pros & Cons of the Amortization Method

Once you have done the initial calculation you do not have to do it again – your payments are usually fixed until age 59½. So this method is easy to administer.

You can also choose from a range of interest rates. The maximum interest rate you can use is 120% of the mid-term Applicable Federal Rate but there is nothing stopping you from using a lower interest rate if you want a lower payment.

In Table 2 an interest rate of 3.43% produces an annual payment of $4,700 for a 45 year old with $100,000. A lower rate such as 2.43% reduces the required payment to $4,009.

Because interest rates have fallen so sharply in recent times, the maximum withdrawal you can take using the amortization method has also fallen sharply.

Note, however, that you can use the rate for *either* of the two months immediately preceding the month in which the distribution begins. This may help you increase or decrease your payment slightly.

## The Annuitization Method

There isn't a huge amount of difference between the amortization method described above and the annuitization method.

Both produce a payment of roughly similar size that remains fixed from year to year. To calculate the amount you can withdraw from your retirement plan each year you need to choose three things:

- An interest rate – same as for the amortization method
- Your account balance – same as for the amortization method
- An annuity factor

An annuity factor is a number calculated by actuaries but you do not need to waste time working it out yourself because there are websites that will do it for you.

Again online calculators like the one on www.72t.net will do it all – just plug in your chosen interest rate, age and account balance.

**Example**

Rick is 40 and his IRA account balance is $100,000. With an interest rate of 3.43% his withdrawal under each of the three methods is:

- Required minimum distribution $2,294
- Amortization method $4,454
- Annuitization method $4,405

The amortization and annuitization methods produce payments of similar size and both are approximately twice as big as the payment from the required minimum distribution method.

### Annuitization Method – Benefits & Drawbacks

In practice you will probably not gain much by using this method over the amortization method.

You should, however, do the calculation using ALL three methods and using the different life expectancy tables to see which produces the most desirable outcome for you.

## Stopping or Changing SEPP Payments

If you start taking SEPP payments from your retirement plan you have to carry on taking them for five years or until you reach age 59½ – whichever lasts longer.

### Example

John is 40 years of age and starts taking substantially equal periodic payments from his IRA. After 5 years he has still not reached age 59½ so must carry on taking money out of his IRA.

Simon is 57 years of age and starts taking substantially equal periodic payments from his IRA. When he reaches age 59½ he will have to carry on taking payments until the five year minimum period is finished.

It is not advisable to stop making payments before the minimum time period is up or to change them in an unapproved way.

If you do this you will have to pay the 10% early withdrawal penalty on every payment you have taken AND you will have to pay interest on this penalty.

Remember only those who use the required minimum distribution method can alter their payments each year by plugging in a new life expectancy figure and account balance.

**Example**

Bill begins taking a SEPP payment of $5,000 per year at age 40. Five years later he stops.

Because he has not reached age 59½ all of his withdrawals are disallowed and he will have to pay the 10% penalty on the entire amount:

$5,000 x 5 years x 10% = $2,500

He will also have to pay interest on the 10% penalty.

For example, for the distribution he took at age 40 the 10% penalty is $500. He will have to pay five years of interest on $500 at the IRS underpayment interest rate, currently 5%.

For the distribution he took age 41 he will have to pay 4 years of interest on $500… and so on.

## When You Can Stop or Alter Your Payments

If you die, become disabled or if your IRA runs out of money you do not have to continue taking SEPPs.

You may also be able to make a one time change to your calculation method.

Only those using the amortization or annuitization method can do this and they have to switch to the required minimum distribution method.

You can only do this once. Once you switch you cannot switch back to the amortization or annuitization method again.

Switching to the required minimum distribution method would normally produce a lower payment but could result in a higher payment if:

- Your IRA account balance has grown significantly.

- Your SEPP plan has been running for many years and your life expectancy is therefore lower.

Note that if you are currently using the required minimum distribution method you cannot switch to the amortization or annuitization methods.

## The Benefit of Multiple IRA Accounts

If you only have one IRA account and start taking substantially equal periodic payments you cannot withdraw any extra money from that account.

The danger then is that you leave yourself nothing extra for emergencies.

For example, you will not be able to make any other penalty free withdrawals to pay for medical expenses, education costs or a first-time home purchase.

So if you have more than one IRA account you should consider excluding one or more of them from your SEPP plan.

This is possible because each of your IRA accounts is treated individually – when you start taking substantially equal periodic payments you do not have to include all of your IRA accounts.

If you only have one IRA account you should consider splitting it first and using one portion for your SEPP plan and the second portion to cover any emergency withdrawals.

Another problem of having only one IRA account is that you cannot make any new tax deductible contributions if you are taking substantially equal periodic payments.

There is, however, nothing stopping you from establishing a new IRA account and making tax deductible contributions.

## A Final Word on SEPPs

Taking substantially equal periodic payments could prove extremely helpful if you do not qualify for any of the other exceptions to the 10% early distribution tax.

However, there are at least two big drawbacks:

- You can only withdraw a small percentage of your IRA account each year.
- You have to keep taking payments for at least five years and possibly almost 20 or 30 years if you are only 40 or 30 years of age.

For this reason SEPPs are not an ideal fix if you have short-term financial problems, especially if you are relatively young.

For example, let's say you are 45 years old and require $20,000 urgently to help repay some loans. Let's say you have $100,000 sitting in your IRA account and are unable to obtain the money anywhere else.

If you use all of your IRA account to set up a SEPP plan the most you will be able to withdraw in one year is $4,700 (based on the current interest rate at the time of writing). You will have to pay tax on this money and if your tax rate is 25% that will leave you with just $3,525.

This means you will have to wait over five years to get your hands on the $20,000 you need!

And once your financial emergency is over you will have to continue pulling money out of your plan until you are 59½ – all of this money could have been growing tax free inside your IRA.

For this reason SEPPs are only really suitable for those who require *ongoing* financial assistance.

For example, a SEPP plan could be suitable for someone who wants to retire early or someone with a new business that needs financial support for several years, or someone who needs ongoing help with loan repayments.

If you are relatively young and require a single cash lump sum quickly, and withdrawing money from your IRA is the only option, you may be better off taking the 10% tax hit... in the long run it may prove less costly than withdrawing money out of a tax sheltered retirement account for many years.

# 3

# *Other Tax-Free IRA Withdrawals*

## Excess Contributions

If you contribute more money to your IRA than you are entitled to for the year, you can withdraw it before your tax return is due (including extensions).

You will not have to pay the 10% additional tax.

You will also have to withdraw any earnings those contributions have generated and these will be subject to income tax and also the 10% tax unless you qualify for one of the exceptions listed in Chapter 1 (medical expenses, educations costs etc).

## Your Basis is Tax Free

Most people make tax deductible contributions to their traditional IRA, but if you made any contributions that were not deductible you will have accumulated "basis" in your plan.

Basis can be taken out tax free (which is only fair because you didn't enjoy any tax benefit when you put the money in!) You do not have to pay income tax or the 10% additional tax on these amounts.

Unfortunately you cannot extract your tax-free basis in one go – it has to be taken out pro rata. So if you withdraw any money, some of it will be taxable and some of it will be tax free.

### Example

Robert made non-deductible contributions of $6,000 to his IRA, so he has $6,000 of basis. His IRA account is valued at $26,000 on December 31 and he withdrew $4,000 during the year to pay some of the family's bills.

Although he has $5,000 of basis his withdrawal is only partially tax free. To calculate the tax free portion we do the following.

- Add the $4,000 withdrawal to the $26,000 end of year balance which comes to $30,000
- Divide Robert's $6,000 basis by $30,000
- The result is 20%

This means Robert will not have to pay tax on 20% of his $4,000 distribution – so $800 will be tax free.

In order to ensure that you are entitled to tax-free treatment you must file IRS Form 8606 in any year that you add basis to your IRA. You also have to file this form for any year that distributions are made if you have made non-deductible contributions.

If you do not file this form you could end up paying a penalty – $50 for each failure to file.

## IRA Loans

Loans are allowed from 401(k) plans but not from IRAs.

If a loan is taken from an IRA it will cease to exist and the entire value will be included in your income and taxed.

There is one small exception to this rule but you have to be very careful about using it.

The IRS lets you take money out of your IRA as long as you repay it within 60 days.

If you do not repay the money on time you will have to pay income tax on it and, if you are under 59½, there is also the 10% penalty.

The 60-day concession is designed for IRA investors who want to move money from one account to another. So if you use the money for some other purpose and fail to meet the deadline, the IRS will not show you much mercy.

There have been instances where IRA accounts have been used to buy a home before an existing one was sold only to see the 60 day rule being breached. The IRS has shown no clemency in these circumstances.

Only if you intend to do a rollover will they cut you some slack if the 60 day limit is breached, for example if you were given bad advice.

You can only move funds from one IRA to another once every 12 months. So if you need to take money out, make sure you use an account that has not been involved in a transfer recently – otherwise you have to pay tax on the withdrawal.

# 4

# *Tapping Your Roth IRA*

## Introduction

Contributions to traditional IRAs are tax deductible and paid out of pre-tax dollars. Contributions to Roth IRAs are not deductible – your contributions are paid out of after-tax dollars.

However, when you reach age 59½ any money you withdraw from your Roth IRA will normally be tax free, whereas you have to pay income tax on traditional IRA withdrawals.

But what happens if you want to withdraw money *early* from a Roth IRA, for example if you lose your job or have another financial emergency? Do you have to pay income tax? And what about the 10% early withdrawal penalty?

To answer these questions we have to divide your Roth IRA account into two parts:

- Your contributions
- Your investment returns

## Your Roth IRA Contributions

The good news is the money you contribute to a Roth IRA can be withdrawn *at any time* tax free – you do not have to pay income tax or the 10% penalty on your original contributions.

It doesn't matter how long the money has been sitting there, how old you are or what you use it for.

Furthermore, the IRS treats any money you withdraw from a Roth IRA as tax-free contributions until these amounts have been completely exhausted.

For example, let's say you have $10,000 sitting in a Roth IRA – $8,000 of contributions and $2,000 of interest on those contributions.

If you now withdraw $8,000 the entire amount will be treated as your tax-free contributions – you do not have to treat any of the money as earnings.

This favorable tax treatment makes Roth IRAs an excellent place to store emergency cash. Remember with traditional IRAs you can only withdraw money penalty free if it is used for specific reasons, for example to pay certain medical expenses or to buy your first home.

You can avoid the 10% penalty by taking substantially equal periodic payments (SEPPs) and these withdrawals can be used for any purpose.

However, these payment plans only allow you to extract a small amount each year and you have to keep withdrawing for at least five years and possibly a lot longer until you reach age 59½. By this time your financial emergency will probably be a distant memory!

Even if you avoid the 10% tax on withdrawals from your traditional IRA you will still have to pay normal income tax. But if you are experiencing financial hardship and need to tap your retirement savings, the last thing you want is to pay a quarter or a third of this money to the IRS.

With your Roth IRA contributions, however, you can withdraw the entire amount tax free at any time.

### Example

Samantha contributed $8,000 to a Roth IRA in 2007 and 2008. She loses her job in 2009 and needs some emergency cash to pay bills until she gets another job.

She withdraws all of her contributions and now has a tax-free lump sum of $8,000 to help pay her mortgage, grocery bills and other day to day expenses.

## Roth IRA Earnings

The money you contribute to your Roth IRA will hopefully grow over time. If you invest it in bonds or CDs it will produce interest and if you invest it in stocks it will earn dividends and hopefully produce healthy capital gains.

What happens if you want to withdraw both your contributions **and** your earnings?

Your earnings distributions are tax free as long as they are "qualified distributions".

So what is a qualified distribution? A qualified distribution has to meet two requirements:

## Requirement 1 – The 5 Year Rule

The first thing you have to remember is the five-year rule. Withdrawals of earnings are only tax free if your first Roth IRA account is at least five years old.

The five year period only relates to your *first* contribution to your first Roth IRA account. Once the five year period is up it is complete for *all* your contributions and *all* your Roth IRA accounts.

The five year period may actually last less than five calendar years because the five year period starts on January 1 of the tax year of your first contribution.

## Example

Steve opened a Roth IRA in December 2005. The five year period will be complete on January 1 2010 – just 4 years later.

If Steve starts making withdrawals of earnings before this date he will have to pay income tax and possibly the 10% penalty. Remember, however, that he can take out his contributions tax free at any time.

The five year period may last even less time if you make a contribution after the tax year has ended.

For example, you have until April 15 2010 to make a contribution for the 2009 tax year.

### Example

Let's say Steve made his Roth IRA contribution for the 2005 tax year at the beginning of April 2006. Again the five year period will be complete on January 1 2010 – three years and 9 months later.

### Requirement 2

If you pass the five-year test you are not done yet – your Roth IRA earnings withdrawals will only count as tax-free qualified distributions if:

- You are 59½ or older
- You have become disabled or the distribution is to your beneficiary when you die.
- You use the money to purchase a home and you are a first-time homebuyer (the lifetime limit for this is $10,000). Qualified family members include you, your spouse, children, grandchildren and parents.

If we ignore the last two bullet points which only apply to a small number of people, the rule for Roth IRAs can be summarized as follows:

**Roth IRA <u>earnings</u> distributions are only tax free if your account is at least five years old and you have reached age 59½.**

If you do not pass this test your distributions will be non-qualified and income tax will be payable.

The next question is, will the 10% additional tax also be payable?

We will answer this question shortly but, at the risk of sounding like a broken record, I would like to emphasize once again that your *contributions* to a Roth IRA can always be withdrawn tax free.

**Example**

Wendy is 35 years old and has been contributing to a Roth IRA for 7 years. She has made contributions of $15,000 and growth on those contributions comes to $3,000. She needs cash urgently and decides to tap her Roth IRA.

She can withdraw all of her $15,000 contributions without having to pay income tax or the 10% penalty tax.

The remaining $3,000 of earnings will, however, be subject to regular income tax unless the money was used for a first-time home purchase.

Why are her earnings taxable? Although she meets requirement 1 because her account is over five years old, she is not 59½ years of age, so her distribution is non qualified.

She may also have to pay the 10% additional tax, if she does not qualify for one of the exceptions discussed below.

### The 10% Additional Tax

To recap, Roth IRA *earnings* distributions are qualified and completely tax free if your account is at least five years old and you have reached age 59½.

(They are also qualified and tax free if your account is at least five years old and the money is withdrawn because of death, disability or to buy your first home).

If you make a nonqualified distribution of earnings you will have to pay income tax on it.

You will also have to pay the 10% early withdrawal penalty unless you are over 59½ years of age or use the money for:

- Payouts on death or disability.
- Substantially equal periodic payments.
- Unreimbursed medical expenses that exceed 7½% of your adjusted gross income.
- Medical insurance premiums after you have received unemployment compensation for more than 12 weeks.
- Qualified higher education costs for you or an eligible family member.
- A first-time home purchase ($10,000 lifetime limit).
- Paying back taxes because of an IRS levy.

These are the same as the early withdrawal exceptions for traditional IRAs (see Chapter 1).

**Example**

Marisa is 45, her Roth IRA account is over five years old and is valued at $20,000:

- $15,000 of contributions, and
- $5,000 of earnings

She needs to withdraw the entire amount to pay off some loans. How much tax will she pay?

The $15,000 in contributions can be taken tax free.

She will have to pay income tax on the $5,000 of earnings because she is not 59½ and is not using the money for a first-time home purchase.

She will also have to pay the 10% early withdrawal tax on these earnings ($500) because she does not qualify for any of the exceptions listed above.

If she used the money for one of the exception reasons listed above she would still pay income tax on her earnings but not the 10% additional tax.

An exception to this would be $10,000 taken out for a first-time home purchase. This withdrawal would be regarded as qualified and escape both income tax and the 10% additional tax.

If her Roth IRA was less than five years old, however, any withdrawal for a first-time home purchase, would be nonqualified and regular income tax would be payable (but not the 10% additional tax).

Phew!

## IRA Conversions

If your Roth IRA account contains a mixture of conversions and contributions the rules for early withdrawals get a bit more tricky.

A Roth IRA conversion takes place if you convert a traditional IRA into a Roth IRA.

When you do this you usually have to pay income tax on all the money transferred.

If you then withdraw any of this money within five years, that money will be subject to the 10% early withdrawal tax if you are under 59½ and do not qualify for one of the exceptions (such as medical expenses).

### Example

Jim is 45 and has $20,000 in his traditional IRA. He converts to a Roth IRA and pays income tax on the entire $20,000. Two years later he withdraws $10,000 to buy a car for his son.

He doesn't have to pay income tax because he paid that when he did the conversion. However, because he is under 59½ and withdrew the money within 5 years of making the conversion, he has to pay the 10% penalty tax on $10,000 – $1,000.

The important thing to remember is that there are different five-year holding periods for conversions and contributions. Even if your contribution holding period has been completed, your conversion holding period also has to be completed.

Furthermore, every conversion you make from a traditional IRA to a Roth IRA will have its own individual five year holding period.

If some of your original contributions to your traditional IRA were not deductible you do not pay income tax on these amounts when you convert to a Roth IRA. You will then not have to pay the 10% penalty when you withdraw them.

## Ordering Your Withdrawals

If you have more than one Roth IRA account the IRS treats them as a single account when it comes to taking withdrawals.

Withdrawals from a Roth IRA are treated as taking place in a specific order, regardless of which account you tap.

Fortunately the order they force you to use is also the most favorable from a tax perspective. Roth distributions are made in the following order (once money from one source has been distributed, the money from the next source is distributed):

- Regular Roth IRA contributions
- Taxable traditional IRA conversions
- Nontaxable traditional IRA conversions
- Earnings on all Roth IRAs

**Example**

Jane set up her first Roth in 2004 and started contributing $1,000 per year. In 2008 she converted her traditional IRA into a Roth IRA. It's now 2009 and Jane is 45 years old and her Roth IRA account contains the following money:

| | |
|---|---|
| $5,000 | Roth IRA contributions (2004-2008) |
| $25,000 | Taxable conversion from 2008 |
| $5,000 | Non-taxable conversion from 2008 |
| $2,500 | Earnings on contributions & conversions |

She want to withdraw money from her Roth IRA. How much tax she pays depends on how much money she withdraws:

**$5,000 Withdrawal**

According to the ordering rules regular Roth IRA contributions are distributed first. Because she made $5,000 of contributions this withdrawal will be completely tax free: no income tax or 10% early distribution tax.

**$10,000 Withdrawal**

The first $5,000 comes from regular Roth IRA contributions and is completely tax free. The next $5,000 comes from the taxable part of her traditional IRA conversion. Income tax was paid when the conversion took place so does not have to be paid again.

She will, however, have to pay the 10% early distribution tax on this $5,000 because the conversion took place less than five years ago.

She will not, however, have to pay the 10% tax if she qualifies for one of the exceptions listed above (after age 59½, death or disability, medical expenses, educations costs, first-time home purchase, IRS levy, education costs, medical insurance premiums).

If the conversion had taken place more than five years ago she would not have to pay this 10% tax.

### $35,000 Withdrawal

Again the first $5,000 would be completely tax free. The next $25,000 would come from her taxable conversion so no income tax would be payable but she will have to pay the 10% additional tax on this money unless she qualifies for one of the exceptions.

The final $5,000 comes from the nontaxable part of her conversion. This money will not be subject to either income tax or the 10% additional tax because no deduction was given when this money was contributed to the traditional IRA.

### $37,500 Withdrawal

The first $35,000 will be treated as above. The final $2,500 comes out of Jane's earnings. Although Jane has had her IRA for five years her earnings distribution counts as nonqualified and she will have to pay income tax on it.

It would only count as qualified if she was over 59½ or the money was taken out on account of death or disability or for a first-time home purchase.

She will also have to pay the 10% early-distribution tax unless one of the exceptions applies.

# 5

# Tapping Your 401(k)

## Introduction

If you want to get your hands on your 401(k) money early you have two options:

- Take a loan, which has to be repaid.
- Apply for a hardship withdrawal, which does not have to be repaid.

A loan normally has to be taken before you will be allowed to take a permanent withdrawal.

Loans can be taken for any reason but permanent withdrawals are only allowed if you are experiencing "financial hardship". The IRS provides a list of what it considers appropriate hardship withdrawals.

With IRAs you never have to prove hardship. Money can be taken out at any time and for any reason, as long as you are prepared to pay the 10% additional tax if you do not qualify for one of the exceptions (medical expenses, education costs etc).

With 401(k) plans you also have to pay the 10% additional tax, unless you are 59½ or an exception applies. The 401(k) exceptions are similar to the IRA ones but there are some differences, as we will see shortly.

With 401(k) plans, as with traditional IRAs, you always have to pay income tax on permanent withdrawals.

## Borrowing from Your 401(k)

Let's kick off with the 401(k) loan rules because you normally cannot take a hardship withdrawal until you have borrowed as much as you can from your plan.

The nice thing about taking a loan from your 401(k) is you do not have to pay Federal or state income tax or the 10% additional tax. These taxes can eat up almost $0.50c out of every $1 you withdraw.

Most plans allow you to borrow money for any reason, others are a bit more restrictive. For example, some plans will only let you borrow to pay unreimbursed medical expenses, education costs, or to prevent a home foreclosure.

You may also need your spouse's consent to take a loan from your 401(k).

Repayment is usually made through payroll deductions and although you will have to pay interest, you pay it to yourself, instead of to a bank!

The rate charged is usually the prime rate plus 1 or 2 percentage points. That interest can then compound tax free inside the plan until you retire.

The IRS will not treat your loan as a taxable distribution from your 401(k) as long as it meets certain criteria.

For starters the loan cannot exceed the *smaller* of:

- $50,000
- Half your account balance

When we talk about account balance we're talking about your "vested" account balance – your nonforfeitable accrued benefits.

Furthermore, everyone can borrow *at least* $10,000, providing you have this much money in your account.

**Example**

Jane's 401(k) vested account balance is $60,000 and she wants to take a loan. The maximum loan she can take is the lesser of:

- $50,000
- Half her account balance - $30,000

So Jane's loan is limited to $30,000.

### Example

Ricardo's nonforfeitable 401(k) account balance is $15,000. The maximum loan he can take is the lesser of:

- $50,000
- Half his account balance - $7,500

However, because everyone can borrow up to $10,000, Ricardo's loan is limited to $10,000, not $7,500.

Loans must always be repaid within 5 years unless you use the money to buy your main home. The IRS does not specify how long you have got to repay a home loan but up to 30 years would probably be acceptable, although your employer may require repayment within 10 to 15 years.

The loan must be repaid using "substantially level payments" – at least one every three months over the life of the loan.

### Multiple Loans

You have to reduce the $50,000 amount if you had an outstanding loan in the last 12 months.

The $50,000 limit is reduced by your highest outstanding loan balance in the last 12 months minus the outstanding balance on the date you took out the new loan.

This is best illustrated with an example.

**Example**

Stan's vested balance in his 401(k) plan is $120,000. He borrows $20,000 from his plan in March. By November of the same year he has repaid $5,000 but unfortunately has to borrow more money.

How much can he now borrow?

First of all we reduce the $50,000 limit by the amount he still owes – $15,000. That leaves $35,000.

The $35,000 is then reduced by his highest outstanding loan balance in the last 12 months ($20,000), *minus* the outstanding balance on the date he took the new loan ($15,000). This comes to $5,000.

So the $35,000 is further reduced by $5,000 which leaves $30,000, the maximum he can now borrow.

## Borrowing Danger

Beware that if you lose or leave your job you will probably have to repay the loan within 30 to 90 days.

If you do not repay the loan on time it will be treated as an early withdrawal and you will have to pay income tax and the 10% penalty on the whole amount.

For this reason you should not consider borrowing from your 401(k) plan if you are planning to quit your job or if there is a danger that you will lose it and you do not have sufficient resources to repay the loan quickly.

## Advantages and Disadvantages of Loans

Advantages:

- There is no income tax or extra 10% tax.
- No credit check is required and 401(k) loans are not reported to credit agencies.
- The interest rate is usually low.
- The interest is paid to yourself instead of a bank and grows tax free inside your plan.
- It is easy to borrow and will often require little more than completing a short form and signing a repayment agreement.

Disadvantages:

- The money you borrow from your plan will not be generating tax-free interest, dividends and capital gains while it is outside your plan.
- If you do not repay the loan it will become a taxable distribution, resulting in income tax and possibly the 10% additional tax on the entire amount.
- You may have to pay a loan fee.
- Interest is not tax deductible, even if the loan is used to buy your main home.
- Loan repayments have to be made out of after-tax dollars.

## Hardship Withdrawals

The first question you have to answer is, am I eligible for a permanent hardship withdrawal?

Remember with 401(k) plans you are not always entitled to pull out money, even if you are prepared to pay the 10% additional tax.

Permanent withdrawals are only allowed if you are experiencing "financial hardship". This can be difficult to quantify but the IRS regards the following as legitimate expenses:

- Unreimbursed medical bills for you, your spouse or dependents.
- Expenses for buying your "principal residence" (but not for regular mortgage payments).
- College tuition and related expenses for the next 12 months for you, your spouse, dependents or children who are no longer dependents.
- Payments to prevent foreclosure of your principal residence or eviction from your home.
- Repairs to your primary residence.
- Funeral expenses for your parents, spouse or other family member.

Although the IRS allows you to withdraw money for the reasons listed above, that doesn't mean your employer will!

Each plan has different rules and some are more strict than others.

For example, some plans will tolerate withdrawals to cover medical expenses but not the purchase of a home.

Some plans do not allow you to take out money even if you have reached age 59½ – you have to wait until your employment comes to an end.

The hardship can be suffered by you, your spouse or dependents. Furthermore, in terms of the 2006 Pension Protection Act the hardship can also be suffered by your non-spouse or non-dependent beneficiary.

## You Must Have No Other Assets

If you, your spouse or minor children have assets, such as a vacation home, that could be sold instead of taking a hardship withdrawal, the IRS does not consider a distribution from your 401(k) plan necessary.

You only qualify for a hardship withdrawal if you cannot find the money anywhere else, including taking a loan from the plan.

If you receive a hardship distribution you will generally not be allowed to make any new contributions to your 401(k) plan for 6 months. This means you may also lose out on matching contributions from your employer. So there are serious costs to consider.

### Proving Hardship

Employees are sometimes required to provide proof of hardship but most plans do not probe heavily into your affairs and will take your word for it.

As long as you need money for one of the six reasons listed above many plan administrators are happy to accept your case for a distribution.

### Limits on Hardship Distributions

A retirement plan will generally allow hardship distributions only up to the amount of your elective contributions.

Your employer's qualified matching contributions and any earnings on the account must usually remain in the plan.

Even if your plan does allow you to make a hardship distribution, remember that you will still have to pay income tax on the entire amount.

The plan administrator will withhold these taxes (this isn't the case with IRAs).

## 401(k) Exceptions

Although the IRS allows you to take hardship distributions for the reasons listed above, you will only escape the 10% additional tax if you qualify for one of the following exceptions:

- You are age 59½ or older.
- You become disabled.
- The distribution is made to a beneficiary when you die.
- You have medical expenses exceeding 7.5% of your AGI, even if you don't itemize.
- You have to pay alimony or child support as part of a QDRO.
- You quit your job or get laid off and you are at least 55 years old.
- You quit your job or get laid off and set up a series of substantially equal periodic payments (SEPPs) from your 401(k). These must last five years or until your reach 59½, whichever is longer.
- The money is used to pay a Federal tax levy

These 401(k) exceptions are similar to the IRA ones we discussed in Chapter 1. However, there are some important differences.

Let's take a closer look at each of them:

**When You Turn 59½**

As with IRAs, withdrawals after age 59½ escape the 10% additional tax, withdrawals before age 59½ are subject to the 10% tax, unless you qualify for one of the other exceptions listed above.

Note that you have to be at least 59½ when you make the withdrawal. If you only reach age 59½ later in the year that is not acceptable.

## When You Die

As with IRAs, if you die before reaching age 59½, your beneficiary will not have to pay the 10% early withdrawal penalty.

It is also possible for your spouse-beneficiary to roll over a distribution from your retirement plan or IRA to his or her retirement plan or IRA.

## Permanent Disability

As with IRAs, if you become permanently disabled money can be withdrawn from your 401(k) without the 10% penalty.

If a physician decides that due to mental or physical disability you are unable to do the type of work you were doing before you were disabled, you are allowed to take penalty-free distributions from your 401(k).

The disability must be expected to last *permanently* or result in your death.

These distributions can be used for any purpose.

## Medical Expenses

As with IRAs, if you have non-reimbursed medical expenses you can make penalty-free 401(k) withdrawals to cover the costs.

The expenses can be for you, your spouse or dependent.

Your withdrawals are only penalty free to the extent your medical expenses exceed 7.5% of your adjusted gross income (AGI).

## Example

Tom has AGI of $50,000 and medical expenses of $5,000, paid using a distribution from his 401(k) plan.

His calculation looks like this:

| | |
|---|---|
| Adjusted gross income | $50,000 |
| Medical expenses | $5,000 |
| 7.5% AGI | $3,750 |
| Excess | $1,250 |

Only $1,250 will avoid the 10% penalty. The 10% penalty is payable on the remaining $3,750. Remember also that regular income tax also has to be paid on the entire $5,000.

**Tax Busting Tip!**

The medical expenses exemption is available to everybody, not just those who itemize expenses on their tax returns. If you claim the standard deduction you still qualify.

**Child Support & Alimony**

If you are paying child support or alimony you can make the payments from your 401(k) and avoid the 10% penalty tax.

However, it is essential the payments are part of a qualified domestic relations order, also known as a QDRO.

If the payments are simply part of a private agreement between you and your ex spouse they will not be exempt from the 10% additional tax.

This exception applies to 401(k) plans but not IRAs. So if you withdraw money from an IRA to pay a QDRO you will have to pay the 10% penalty.

### Age 55 and Over and Leave Job

This exception is available for 401(k) plans but not IRAs.

If you are 55 or older and leave your job the IRS lets you withdraw money from your 401(k). You will still have to pay income tax but will escape the 10% additional tax.

Although the IRS will let you take out money your plan provider may place limits on how much you can withdraw.

This exemption is only relevant if you are aged between 55 and 59½ when you leave your job. When you reach age 59½, of course, the 10% penalty no longer applies.

You do not have to stop working *permanently*. You can still go and work for another employer. All that matters is that you leave the employer who runs the plan you are taking money out of.

You do not have to be 55 on the day you leave your job. All that matters is you reach this age by December 31 of the same year.

But be careful if you leave your job at, say, age 53 and start taking money out of your previous employer's plan after you turn 55. This loophole only works if you turn 55 in the same year you leave your job. Otherwise you will have to pay the 10% penalty!

### Substantially Equal Periodic Payments

Like IRA account holders, members of 401(k) plans can also take substantially equal periodic payments and avoid the 10% additional tax.

There is, however, one big difference: with an IRA you can take SEPPs at any time but with 401(k)s you can only take SEPPs if you are no longer employed by the sponsoring company.

See Chapter 2 for a full discussion of SEPPs.

### Federal Tax Levy

As with IRAs, the 10% penalty is waived if money is paid out of your 401(k) as a result on an IRS levy. Note you will not qualify for this exception if you voluntarily withdraw the money from your plan to pay taxes in order to avoid a levy.

## IRAs vs 401(k)s

IRA account holders, but not 401(k) plan members, can avoid the 10% additional tax if they withdraw money to pay for certain:

- Education expenses
- Medical insurance premiums
- First-time home purchase costs

See Chapter 1 for more information on these exceptions.

However, 401(k) plan members can avoid the 10% additional tax on money withdrawn to pay certain:

- Court ordered child support and alimony
- Distributions at age 55 or older

IRA account holders do not qualify for these two exceptions.

You can withdraw money from both your IRA or your 401(k) without the 10% additional tax if you are over age 59½ or if:

- You become disabled.
- The distributions is to your beneficiaries when you die.
- You take substantially equal periodic payments (SEPPs).
- You have unreimbursed medical expenses in excess of 7.5% of your adjusted gross income.
- The distribution is used to pay an IRS levy.

Often it is worth considering withdrawing funds from your IRA instead of your 401(k). For example, both types of plan let you withdraw money to pay expenses related to a home purchase or to pay college tuition fees.

However, the big difference is that there is no 10% penalty if the funds come from your IRA (although the amount for home purchase is limited to $10,000 and that is a lifetime limit).

## Tax Busting Tip!

If you want to withdraw up to $10,000 for a first-time home purchase you can save more tax by tapping a Roth IRA instead of a traditional IRA or 401(k) plan.

A distribution from a 401(k) plan is permitted by the IRS but will incur both income tax and the 10% additional tax.

A distribution from a traditional IRA will escape the 10% additional tax but you will have to pay income tax on the whole amount.

A distribution of earnings from a Roth IRA will escape both income tax and the 10% additional tax, providing your account is at least five years old. And of course your contributions can always be taken tax free.

# 6

# *Reporting Early IRA and 401(k) Distributions*

## Introduction

If you take money out of your retirement plan, the custodian company will send you and the IRS a copy of Form 1099-R (to view a sample form type "IRS Form 1099-R into a search engine like Google).

You must attach this form to your tax return if any tax was withheld from the distribution.

If no tax was withheld you do not have to attach it.

## Form 5329

There's another form that pertains to additional taxes on IRAs and other qualified plans – IRS Form 5329.

To view this form type "IRS Form 5329" into a search engine like Google and to read the instructions which accompany this form type in "IRS Instruction 5329".

If the number "1" is shown in Box 7 of the 1099-R and you owe the 10% additional tax on the distribution you do not have to file Form 5329.

Instead you should multiply the taxable amount of the distribution by 10% and enter the result in line 59 of your Form 1040 tax return – *Additional tax on IRAs, other qualified retirement plans, etc.*

The amount subject to regular income tax goes on line 15 (if it's an IRA) or 16 if it's another retirement plan.

You do, however, have to file Form 5329 if:

- You received an early distribution from your 401(k) or IRA (but not a Roth IRA) and the number "1" is not shown in Box 7 of your 1099-R.

- You qualify for one of the exceptions to the 10% additional tax and the number "1" appears in Box 7 of the Form 1099-R you received.

- You qualify for one of the exceptions to the 10% additional tax but Box 7 does not indicate that an exception applies.

- You received an early distribution from a Roth IRA.

This is not necessarily a complete list so I would recommend reading the instructions for Form 5329.

## Substantially Equal Periodic Payments

If you receive substantially equal periodic payments from your retirement plan you will receive Form 1099-R from the plan custodian.

If the form contains the number "2" in Box 7 you do not need to file Form 5329 because this code means that you qualify for an exception to the 10% additional tax.

You will however have to report your payments on your tax return.

If your Form 1099-R does not contain "2" in Box 7 you will have to complete Form 5329 to claim the exception.

# Appendix 1
# Single Life Expectancy

| Age | LE | Age | LE | Age | | | |
|---|---|---|---|---|---|---|---|
| 0 | 82.4 | 28 | 55.3 | 56 | 28.7 | 84 | 8.1 |
| 1 | 81.6 | 29 | 54.3 | 57 | 27.9 | 85 | 7.6 |
| 2 | 80.6 | 30 | 53.3 | 58 | 27 | 86 | 7.1 |
| 3 | 79.7 | 31 | 52.4 | 59 | 26.1 | 87 | 6.7 |
| 4 | 78.7 | 32 | 51.4 | 60 | 25.2 | 88 | 6.3 |
| 5 | 77.7 | 33 | 50.4 | 61 | 24.4 | 89 | 5.9 |
| 6 | 76.7 | 34 | 49.4 | 62 | 23.5 | 90 | 5.5 |
| 7 | 75.8 | 35 | 48.5 | 63 | 22.7 | 91 | 5.2 |
| 8 | 74.8 | 36 | 47.5 | 64 | 21.8 | 92 | 4.9 |
| 9 | 73.8 | 37 | 46.5 | 65 | 21 | 93 | 4.6 |
| 10 | 72.8 | 38 | 45.6 | 66 | 20.2 | 94 | 4.3 |
| 11 | 71.8 | 39 | 44.6 | 67 | 19.4 | 95 | 4.1 |
| 12 | 70.8 | 40 | 43.6 | 68 | 18.6 | 96 | 3.8 |
| 13 | 69.9 | 41 | 42.7 | 69 | 17.8 | 97 | 3.6 |
| 14 | 68.9 | 42 | 41.7 | 70 | 17 | 98 | 3.4 |
| 15 | 67.9 | 43 | 40.7 | 71 | 16.3 | 99 | 3.1 |
| 16 | 66.9 | 44 | 39.8 | 72 | 15.5 | 100 | 2.9 |
| 17 | 66 | 45 | 38.8 | 73 | 14.8 | 101 | 2.7 |
| 18 | 65 | 46 | 37.9 | 74 | 14.1 | 102 | 2.5 |
| 19 | 64 | 47 | 37 | 75 | 13.4 | 103 | 2.3 |
| 20 | 63 | 48 | 36 | 76 | 12.7 | 104 | 2.1 |
| 21 | 62.1 | 49 | 35.1 | 77 | 12.1 | 105 | 1.9 |
| 22 | 61.1 | 50 | 34.2 | 78 | 11.4 | 106 | 1.7 |
| 23 | 60.1 | 51 | 33.3 | 79 | 10.8 | 107 | 1.5 |
| 24 | 59.1 | 52 | 32.3 | 80 | 10.2 | 108 | 1.4 |
| 25 | 58.2 | 53 | 31.4 | 81 | 9.7 | 109 | 1.2 |
| 26 | 57.2 | 54 | 30.5 | 82 | 9.1 | 110 | 1.1 |
| 27 | 56.2 | 55 | 29.6 | 83 | 8.6 | 111 + | 1 |

**New Tax Breaks for Home Sellers**

**By Nick Braun EA PhD**

This brand new book will help you lower you taxes when you sell your home. It also contains the clearest explanation you will find anywhere of the tax rules including the brand new rules introduced in 2008.

## *Taxcafe's Unique Tax Videos*

***Did you know that you can now download Taxcafe products to watch in the comfort of your home?***

*Our unique tax videos are the most enjoyable and easy way to learn the best tax saving strategies.*

*Just sit back, relax, and pay less tax!*

*Each professionally produced video also comes with a FREE book – so you get the best of both worlds!*

*All available for Instant Download ... Start watching in minutes!*

*Find out more at* **www.taxcafe.com**

Printed in the United States
222008BV00004B/2/P

9 781906 888022